The World's **MOST** DANGEROUS JOBS

Bomb and Mine Disposal Officers

By Antony Loveless

CRABTREE
Publishing Company
www.crabtreebooks.com

The World's MOST DANGEROUS Jobs

Editors: Mark Sachner, Adrianna Morganelli
Editorial director: Kathy Middleton
Proofreader: Redbud Editorial
Production coordinator: Margaret Salter
Prepress technician: Margaret Salter
Project director: Ruth Owen
Designer: Elaine Wilkinson
Cover design: Alix Wood

Photo credits:
Department of Defense: cover (top), cover (bottom),
    pages 1, 5, 11, 12, 13, 15, 16, 17, 21, 25, 27, 28, 29
Getty Images: Frank Perry: page 7
Fox Photos: page 8
Antony Loveless: page 18, 23

COVER STORY

◄ **COVER (top)** – An explosion cloud caused when a United States Army EOD team detonated a car bomb during an IED training exercise at Fort Irwin, California.

◄ **COVER (bottom)** – Using a Metallic Mine Detector, a United States marine uses a sweeping motion to cover large areas of ground as he searches for enemy mines.

PAGE 1 – A United States bomb disposal technician assists another technician in putting on a bomb suit and protective helmet.

Library and Archives Canada Cataloguing in Publication

Loveless, Antony
    Bomb and mine disposal officers / Antony Loveless.

(The world's most dangerous jobs)
Includes index.
ISBN 978-0-7787-5095-6 (bound).--ISBN 978-0-7787-5109-0 (pbk.)

    1. Bomb squads--Juvenile literature 2. Bomb reconnaissance--
Juvenile literature 3. Explosive ordnance disposal--Juvenile literature
I. Title. II. Series: World's most dangerous jobs

HV8080 B65 L69 2009   j363.17'98   C2009-903568-5

Library of Congress Cataloging-in-Publication Data

Loveless, Antony.
    Bomb and mine disposal officers / Antony Loveless.
      p. cm. -- (The world's most dangerous jobs)
    Includes index.

    ISBN 978-0-7787-5109-0 (pbk. : alk. paper) -- ISBN 978-0-7787-5095-6
(reinforced library binding : alk. paper)
    1. Bomb squads--Juvenile literature. 2. Bomb reconnaissance--Juvenile
literature. 3. Explosive ordnance disposal--Juvenile literature. I. Title.

    UF860.L68 2010
    363.17'98--dc22
                                        2009022854

Published by CRABTREE PUBLISHING COMPANY in 2010

Published in Canada
Crabtree Publishing
616 Welland Ave.
St. Catharines, ON
L2M 5V6

Published in the United States
Crabtree Publishing
PMB16A
350 Fifth Ave., Suite 3308
New York, NY 10118

Published in the United Kingdom
Crabtree Publishing
Lorna House, Suite 3.03, Lorna Road
Hove, East Sussex, UK
BN3 3EL

Published in Australia
Crabtree Publishing
386 Mt. Alexander Rd.
Ascot Vale (Melbourne)
VIC 3032

CONTENTS

BOMB DISPOSAL

In today's world, most people do not take part in dangerous activities during their day at work. For some people, however, facing danger is very much a part of their working life.

Of all the dangerous jobs in the world, bomb and **mine** disposal has to be one of the most dangerous. Bombs and mines are designed to cause injury and death. An unexploded bomb may still explode unexpectedly, and mines can lay dormant but still be effective and deadly for years.

The nature of terrorism in the 21st century means there is an ever-present danger of a bomb being planted in a busy place, such as a city building or airport. Car bombs and IEDs (Improvised Explosive Devices, or homemade bombs) have become a common attack weapon in places such as Afghanistan. Today, bomb disposal officers are in high demand.

What qualities does it take to be able to walk up to an unexploded bomb or IED, calmly examine it, slowly and carefully remove the cover, and attempt to defuse it? How does it feel to be completely alone when everyone else has taken cover?

A bomb is an explosive device, built in a munitions factory. It is designed to be used by military personnel, normally an air force. An IED (Improvised Explosive Device) is a device like a bomb built by non-military people, such as a terrorist group.

▲ United States Air Force bomb disposal officers carry out a controlled detonation of explosives found in Iraq. They do this to keep the weapons from falling back into enemy hands.

▲ A United States Navy bomb disposal technician searches for mines in Mahmudiyah, Iraq.

THE DANGERS

Many bombs, IEDs, mines, **grenades**, **shells**, and **torpedoes** fail to explode on impact. This means they remain on the battlefield long after the fighting is over.

Sometimes IEDs are planted by terrorists in places where they will harm **civilians**. Occasionally old World War II bombs are found. For example, an unexploded WWII bomb might be dug up in a city during construction work.

It's the job of Bomb Disposal Engineers, or EODs (Explosive Ordnance Disposal engineers), to disarm these devices.

EODs work in war zones. They disarm bombs in civilian areas. They are also experts in counter-terrorist searches—uncovering illegal arms and explosives.

Without question, this is dangerous work. During the period 1969 to 1998, 20 British Army EODs were killed by terrorist bombs during a conflict in Northern Ireland that became known as "The Troubles."

In just two years, 2006 to 2008, the United States Air Force (USAF) lost eight EODs in Iraq. The Purple Heart was awarded to 35 USAF EODs who were wounded or killed. In the same period and conflict, the United States Navy lost 11 EOD personnel and the U.S. Marines lost 12.

Most EODs know someone who was killed disarming a bomb. Most also say that they have had a close call of their own.

The Purple Heart is a military decoration awarded by the United States to U.S. military personnel who have been wounded or killed while serving their country.

▼ Bomb disposal experts pose in Angers, France, in 2004, after they disarmed a 1,100-pound (500-kilogram) World War II bomb. Over 3,500 people were evacuated from the area.

"I'm proud to serve in the Royal Logistics Corps as it's one of the most highly regarded units in the world. Because of our training and our experience in Northern Ireland, Iraq, and Afghanistan, we're looked on throughout the world as the experts in IED Disposal."

James, EOD Officer, British Army Royal Logistics Corps

THE HISTORY OF BOMB DISPOSAL

All of today's EOD operatives, wherever they work in the world, share a common history that leads back to World War II.

During World War II, Germany bombarded the UK with fierce air attacks and bombings during a period called the "Blitz." Some of the bombs, known as "UXBs," failed to explode. This was a tremendous threat to the military and to civilians.

The British Army responded by designing equipment and methods to make these devices safe. After the bombing of Pearl Harbor, Hawaii, in 1941, the U.S. War Department set up its own bomb disposal program and training school with help from the British.

In the early 1970s, a new threat emerged—homemade bombs, or IEDs. During "The Troubles" in Northern Ireland, the British Army's Royal Logistics Corps learned how to deal with IEDs such as **pipe bombs**, **victim-triggered devices**, and **roadside bombs**.

The British Army created a specialist bomb disposal unit called 321EOD. The unit lost many personnel. It became the most decorated peacetime squadron for its acts of bravery in Northern Ireland.

◄ A bomb disposal expert disarms a 12,000-pound (5,450-kg) bomb during World War II.

BOMB DISPOSAL IN THE U.K.

There are EOD operators in the United Kingdom's army, air force, and navy. James is an EOD officer with the British Army's Royal Logistics Corps. Army EODs are called Ammunition Technicians (ATs). James says:

All ATs are soldiers first and foremost. This means that you can only apply to specialize in bomb disposal after you've joined the army and completed all your army training. Once you're a fully trained soldier, you can ask to specialize in bomb disposal and become an AT.

Before you can attend the 'class 2 Ammunition Technician course,' there's a pre-select course that you have to pass. You are assessed for leadership skills and problem solving skills. You also undergo numeracy tests and psychometric evaluation. Psychometric tests assess your personality type—for example, are you calm under pressure? Are you the type of person who pays a great deal of attention to small details?

The basic AT course lasts six months and covers disposal of bombs and mines. You also learn the basics behind IEDs and how to dispose of them. It's only really worthwhile teaching basic IED disposal theory because those who plant IEDs are developing and changing them all the time. No two IED devices will ever be the same.

▼ United States Navy EOD divers examine a naval mine during a training exercise.

Naval mines float just beneath the surface of the ocean. They are often planted during wars to protect harbor entrances. A mine is a hazard to a ship because it can blow a hole in the ship and cause it to sink.

BOMB DISPOSAL IN THE U.S.

In the United States, many EOD technicians are attached to law enforcement agencies. Most large police departments have a bomb disposal team. So do government law enforcement agencies such as the FBI (Federal Bureau of Investigation). In some cities, there are EOD teams formed by fire departments.

The U.S. Army's EOD teams deal with all munitions incidents within the confines of military bases and in war zones. Sometimes they will deal with a bomb incident outside of the base if EODs from another agency are not available.

▼ This explosion cloud was caused when a United States Army EOD team detonated a car bomb during an IED training exercise at Fort Irwin, California.

All EOD technicians in the United States attend the joint U.S. Army/FBI Hazardous Devices School at Redstone Arsenal, Alabama. This school is modeled on the International IEDD (IED Disposal) Training School at The British Army School of Ammunition.

The Hazardous Devices School trains EODs in the detection, diagnosis, and disposal of hazardous devices. They are also trained to deal with the aftermath of a bomb—for example, collecting evidence from hazardous devices at the scene of an explosion, or presenting expert witness testimony in court on bombing cases.

▲ A United States Air Force EOD technician searches under a vehicle during a training exercise on Dover Air Force Base, Delaware. He is wearing a bomb suit for protection. The EOD is using a mirror to examine underneath a car for a suspect device.

EOD EQUIPMENT

Disarming an explosive device is a risky business. No amount of armor can protect the wearer against blast injuries sustained at close range.

EODs use basic equipment, such as trowels for careful digging and hi-tech equipment such as remote-controlled robots. They also use equipment that can see inside an explosive device, such as X-ray machines. High performance sensors that are capable of detecting and interpreting sounds, smells, and images from within a bomb are also used.

Once the EODs determine what the device is, and what state it is in, they formulate a procedure to disarm it. Wherever possible, they do this remotely using a robot. Sometimes, however, an EOD must put his or her own life at risk by inspecting a bomb. In this situation, the most valuable asset any EOD has is his or her training and a steady hand!

To inspect a bomb, the EOD puts on a "bomb suit." The suit weighs 81 pounds (37 kg) and is constructed of flame and fragmentation-resistant material similar to a bulletproof vest. Bomb suits are heavy and hot to wear, but they increase an EOD's chances of survival should a device explode.

EODs wear a helmet made of a hard, strong material called Kevlar. The helmet has a two-inch-thick (five-centimeter-thick) transparent visor.

▲ A United States Air Force EOD wearing a bomb suit performs an X-ray test using a Portable Digital X-Ray Imaging System.

ROBOT WHEELBARROWS

The aim of any bomb disposal operator is to
disarm the device as remotely as possible.

One of the tools we use for remote operations is the
RCV (Remotely Controlled Vehicle). This is known by
all EODs across the world as the wheelbarrow.
It's an amazing piece of equipment!

Robots can cross any terrain, climb stairs, push
a car, or render safe any suspect device found.

▲ RCVs have cameras, microphones, and sensors to detect if an
explosive device has chemical or nuclear weapons inside it. Here,
a U.S. Navy EOD directs a Talon robot towards an IED device in Iraq.

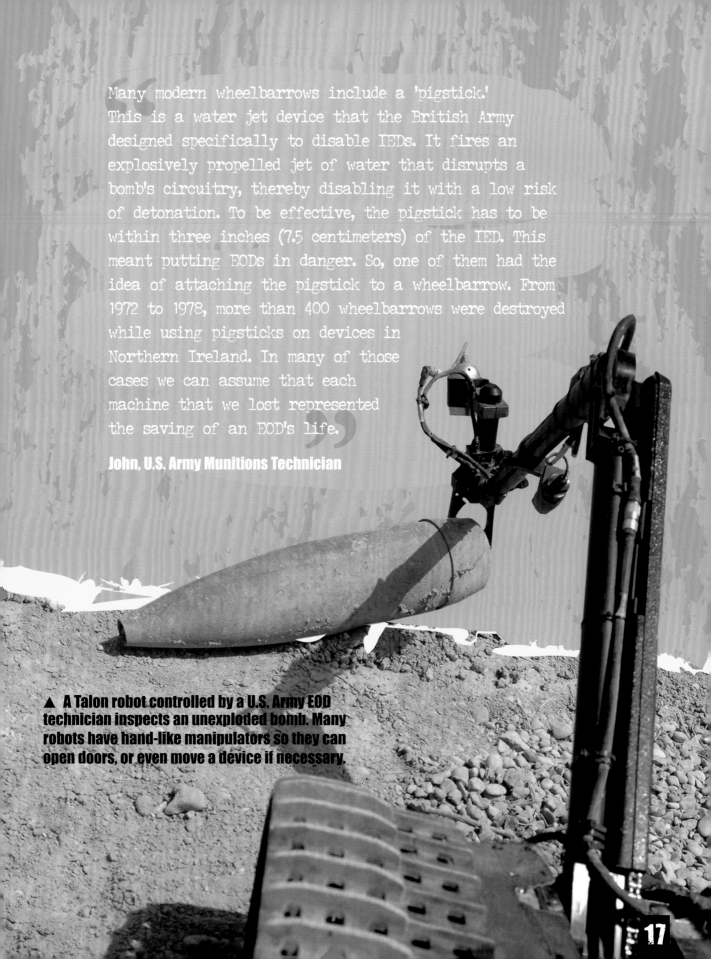

Many modern wheelbarrows include a 'pigstick.'
This is a water jet device that the British Army
designed specifically to disable IEDs. It fires an
explosively propelled jet of water that disrupts a
bomb's circuitry, thereby disabling it with a low risk
of detonation. To be effective, the pigstick has to be
within three inches (7.5 centimeters) of the IED. This
meant putting EODs in danger. So, one of them had the
idea of attaching the pigstick to a wheelbarrow. From
1972 to 1978, more than 400 wheelbarrows were destroyed
while using pigsticks on devices in
Northern Ireland. In many of those
cases we can assume that each
machine that we lost represented
the saving of an EOD's life.

John, U.S. Army Munitions Technician

▲ A Talon robot controlled by a U.S. Army EOD
technician inspects an unexploded bomb. Many
robots have hand-like manipulators so they can
open doors, or even move a device if necessary.

IMPROVISED EXPLOSIVE DEVICES

An explosive device used by a non-military organization, such as a terrorist group, is known as an Improvised Explosive Device, or IED. Callum, a British Army Ammunition Technician, talks about IEDs here:

"Sometimes IEDs include parts of conventional military explosives, such as **artillery rounds**, attached to a detonating mechanism.

IEDs are **really** popular with **terrorists**. We say they are 'dumb weapons' because once they're left in a place there's no risk to the terrorist, but they can kill large numbers of people.

Since the Iraq War started in 2003, IEDs have been used extensively against **coalition forces**. Something like 40 percent of all coalition deaths in Iraq are caused by IEDs.

They've also become **really** popular with **Taliban** forces in Afghanistan. Now, rather than fighting coalition forces in battles where a large number of Taliban were being killed, they are using IEDs.

These devices are often disguised or hidden in everyday objects, such as water barrels. It's very time consuming for British or U.S. patrols to make progress if they think there could be an IED hidden somewhere on their route. IEDs are often placed by the edge of roads to be detonated when vehicles or patrols pass by. So, they're sometimes also known as roadside bombs."

◄ **The crater and devastation left by a massive car bomb that detonated during rush hour in Baghdad, Iraq, in January 2004. Several people were killed and many were injured in the explosion.**

MINES

There are two types of mines—anti-personnel mines and anti-tank mines.

Anti-personnel mines are designed for use against humans. Anti-tank mines have a much larger explosive charge and are designed to be triggered by vehicles such as tanks. Robert, a Royal Air Force (RAF) EOD officer, explains:

"Mines are used to defend land or military positions. They are cheap to produce, small, and easy to lay in large numbers. Once they are deployed, they require no maintenance or human involvement. Mines lie hidden, waiting, until they are stepped on or driven over. Mines can remain a threat for decades if not removed.

Anti-personnel mines are usually pressure activated, so they are triggered when the victim steps on them. They are designed to disable the victim by blowing off their foot or leg. Injuring a member of an opposing force is considered a better tactic than killing them. The opposing force will need to spend time, and use people and equipment, evacuating that soldier or providing medical assistance.

To disarm a mine, the soil is carefully moved away from the side of the mine with a stick-like tool. We try to identify the mine from the side, rather than the top. Once identified, we know how to move the mine and can take it away to be detonated."

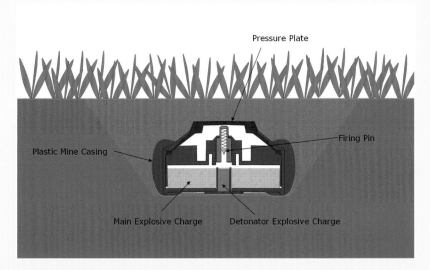

Pressure Plate

Firing Pin

Plastic Mine Casing

Main Explosive Charge

Detonator Explosive Charge

▲ Using a Metallic Mine Detector, a United States marine uses a sweeping motion to cover large areas of ground as he searches for enemy mines.

◄ A cross section of an anti-personnel mine buried under the ground.

BOOBY-TRAPPED BOMBS

Some mines, bombs, and IEDs are booby-trapped. This means they have been specially adapted and protected with something called an **anti-handling device**. Simply lifting up or turning over a booby-trapped bomb or IED can be enough to detonate it.

Booby-trapped devices serve two military purposes. They prevent the reuse of the munition by enemy forces. They also hold up and disrupt bomb disposal or de-mining operations.

Booby traps are homemade weapons, often made from an item such as an artillery shell or grenade or a number of high explosives.

Booby-trapped devices are always hidden or disguised in some way so that they look harmless or can't be seen. For example, enemy forces might place a case of soda pop open on top of a layer of rubble and some explosives. Curious or thirsty soldiers might pick up the soda pop and detonate the explosives. Bombers who place booby traps use people's natural curiosity against them.

▶ **A member of the Royal Air Force Regiment walks ahead of his patrol searching for mines or IEDs near Kandahar Airfield, Afghanistan.**

"It's all about teamwork at the end of the day, and it's important to work seamlessly to get the job done. That's what I love about it. It's methodical, considered, and slow, exacting and thought-provoking work but you get an enormous amount of satisfaction from a job well done. By making bombs safe, you're protecting the lives of people who might otherwise be harmed. It's a tough job, but someone has to do it."

Terry, Royal Air Force (RAF) EOD Operator

THE LONG WALK

Mark is an EOD Officer who was deployed to Iraq at the start of the war in 2003. He was called out to a roadblock on the main supply route near Al Amarah. Here he talks about what it is like to make "the long walk":

This was a key route for **Allied forces**, but local insurgents (people who are fighting Iraq's government) had placed a roadblock across the route on market day. A huge crowd was milling around and there were several suspect objects in place.

A detachment of British Royal Military Police closed the road. We moved the crowds back to a safe point, but it was our job to deal with the munitions, and at this point we didn't know what they were. This was quite early on in the war so we had no equipment with us worth speaking about—no bomb suits or robots. I was wearing just my combat body armor and helmet.

The way we deal with something like that means that one of us—in this case, me—has to approach it on foot and inspect it. It's called 'the long walk' and it's a very lonely place. I've left the safety of the area outside the potential blast zone. Every step I take is putting me closer to the jaws of death. For all we knew, it was a trap and insurgents could have had guns trained on the roadblock. They could have triggered the munitions remotely when I got there—we just didn't know.

"You think of all sorts as you make that walk—your family, what it's like to die, what you did the night before. But for the most part, you're completely focused on the job at hand. When I arrived at the site, I found three devices—a large mine, and two others. My biggest concern was whether they'd been booby-trapped."

Mark's story is continued on the next page...

◄ A United States Navy EOD, on a training exercise at Naval Station Pearl Harbor, records notes about a mine.

A BOOBY TRAP?

Here EOD operator Mark continues his story. Having completed "the long walk," Mark now had to find out if the mines were booby-trapped:

The easiest way to deal with the mines was to dislodge them and see if they exploded. The way we do that is to carefully—very carefully—tie a rope around them and retreat to a safe distance. If you can topple them over without them exploding, then it's pretty safe to assume that they're not booby-trapped and aren't going to suddenly explode.

Once I identified that they were all safe to move, I gathered them up and took them away to a location within our base where they were later blown up.

It's amazing how focused you are when you're dealing with something like that. What stands out for me is the aftermath. It was only when I went back to base afterwards that my body reacted and I was drenched in sweat. It wasn't like being hot normally—we were used to that by then—or the usual perspiration on your brow. My whole body was soaked, top to bottom, my clothes were dripping. I guess it's the release. You're so focused, but afterwards, you think it over and your body reacts.

▶ **Soldiers seek cover as an IED detonates unexpectedly during location and inspection. EOD technicians were called to the scene when an army infantry unit discovered a wire protruding from a mound in the middle of a road southwest of Baghdad, Iraq. There were no injuries or deaths due to the blast.**

SEVEN HOURS...

Terry is an EOD operator who was based in Basra, Iraq. He was called out to disarm a 107 mm Chinese rocket that had failed to explode.

The rocket had penetrated a shelter, gone through another building where someone was watching TV—it went straight past him—and through another building. It finally buried itself beneath the floor of a port-a-cabin in the soft earth.

The accommodation block was at risk until we disarmed it, and so were the lives of everyone who lived there. It had landed without going off, but it might have had a faulty fuze. The slightest movement could have caused the detonator to function, and that would have been it—all over!

We had to follow its route first off, identify where it had landed. Then myself and my No 2 had to go to work on it. We didn't have bomb suits at that time, and a robot wouldn't have been any good in that situation. It was very, very cramped, a really tight space underneath the building. It was a job that only human hands could do."

◄ A U.S. Army EOD clears loose rocks from a 1,000-pound (455-kg) bomb in Afghanistan. Many unexploded bombs litter both Iraq and Afghanistan. They were dropped or planted during previous conflicts.

"We had no idea of what we were dealing with. It might have exploded at any moment. We had to treat it very, very carefully. There was an exclusion zone set up, and just myself and my No 2 were inside the zone. We were flat on our stomachs for over seven hours trying to excavate that rocket.

We used a hand trowel and had to expose the rocket without moving it or causing it to shift. It was painstaking work. A handful of earth at a time, check, move some more, check. Seven hours it took until eventually we were able to disarm it and remove it. Usually, we take unexploded ordnance, such as rockets and bombs, to a safe location, such as a special area within our base, where we explode them."

▲ A fireball and shockwave made by the disposal of seven 1,000-pound (455-kg) bombs in Iraq. A U.S. Army EOD team recovered the bombs and then destroyed them so they could not be used again by the enemy.

IT'S A FACT!

Some bomb suits have advanced features, such as internal cooling, amplified hearing, and communications equipment that connect the EOD to the control area.

Many countries use specially trained dogs to help clear mines. The dogs are able to sniff out explosive chemicals like the TNT that is used in mines.

The Royal Logistics Corp 321EOD unit used the radio call sign "Felix." This was after a famous cartoon cat who had nine lives. Whenever a suspect device was found, the unit was called with the words, "Fetch Felix."

Today, more than 80 countries are affected by unexploded bombs and mines that are leftover from wars. The number of mines that contaminate the world is unknown but there may be millions. It is estimated that every year up to 20,000 people are killed or injured by mines.

If the military needs to move through a heavily mined area quickly, they will use mine-clearing vehicles. These are armored vehicles that are driven through the minefield to explode the mines. The vehicles are able to withstand the blast from the mines with almost no effect.

Bomb & Mine Disposal online

www.army.mod.uk/royalengineers/role/2921.aspx

www.fbi.gov/page2/dec04/hds122004.htm

edition.cnn.com/2007/SHOWBIZ/books/03/06/

excerpt.bomb.squad/index.html

GLOSSARY

allied forces (in Iraq) The forces from 25 different nations (including the United States, United Kingdom, Russia, Australia, South Korea, and Italy) that fought in the Iraq war. Forces that work together in this way are sometimes also called coalition forces.

anti-handling device A device built into a mine or bomb designed to cause it to explode immediately if it is touched. An anti-handling device is different from a booby trap, which is a homemade attempt to entice people to pick up an everyday object, which will then lead to an explosion.

artillery round Ammunition for large weapons, such as cannon, howitzers, and missile launchers.

civilian A person who is not in a branch of the military, such as the army, air force, or navy.

coalition forces Forces from different nations who work together to fight an enemy in a war.

grenade A small bomb that is detonated by a fuse and thrown by hand or shot from a rifle or launcher.

mine An explosive device used to destroy enemy personnel, ships, or vehicles. Mines are often hidden. They are designed to be detonated by contact.

pipe bomb An explosive device contained in a metal pipe.

roadside bomb An IED (Improvised Explosive Device) placed at the side of a road or track. Roadside bombs are usually detonated by remote control when an army patrol passes by.

shell An artillery projectile containing an explosive charge.

Taliban A radical Sunni Muslim organization that governed Afghanistan from 1996 to 2001. It has been fighting a guerrilla war against the current government of Afghanistan and allied forces.

terrorist A person who tries to frighten people or governments into doing what he or she wants by using violence or the threat of violence.

torpedo An underwater projectile launched from a submarine, aircraft, or ship.

victim-triggered device A bomb, mine, or IED (Improvised Explosive Device) that has been booby-trapped.

INDEX

Printed in the USA—BG